The Story of Navaho Weaving

Illustrated with photographs
of blankets in the collection

of the

HEARD MUSEUM
Of Anthropology and Primitive Art

Phoenix, Arizona

by

Kate Peck Kent

Library of Congress Catalogue Number
61-17172

Fifth Printing 1970
Printed at Phoenix, Arizona USA
by McGrew Printing & Lithographing Co.

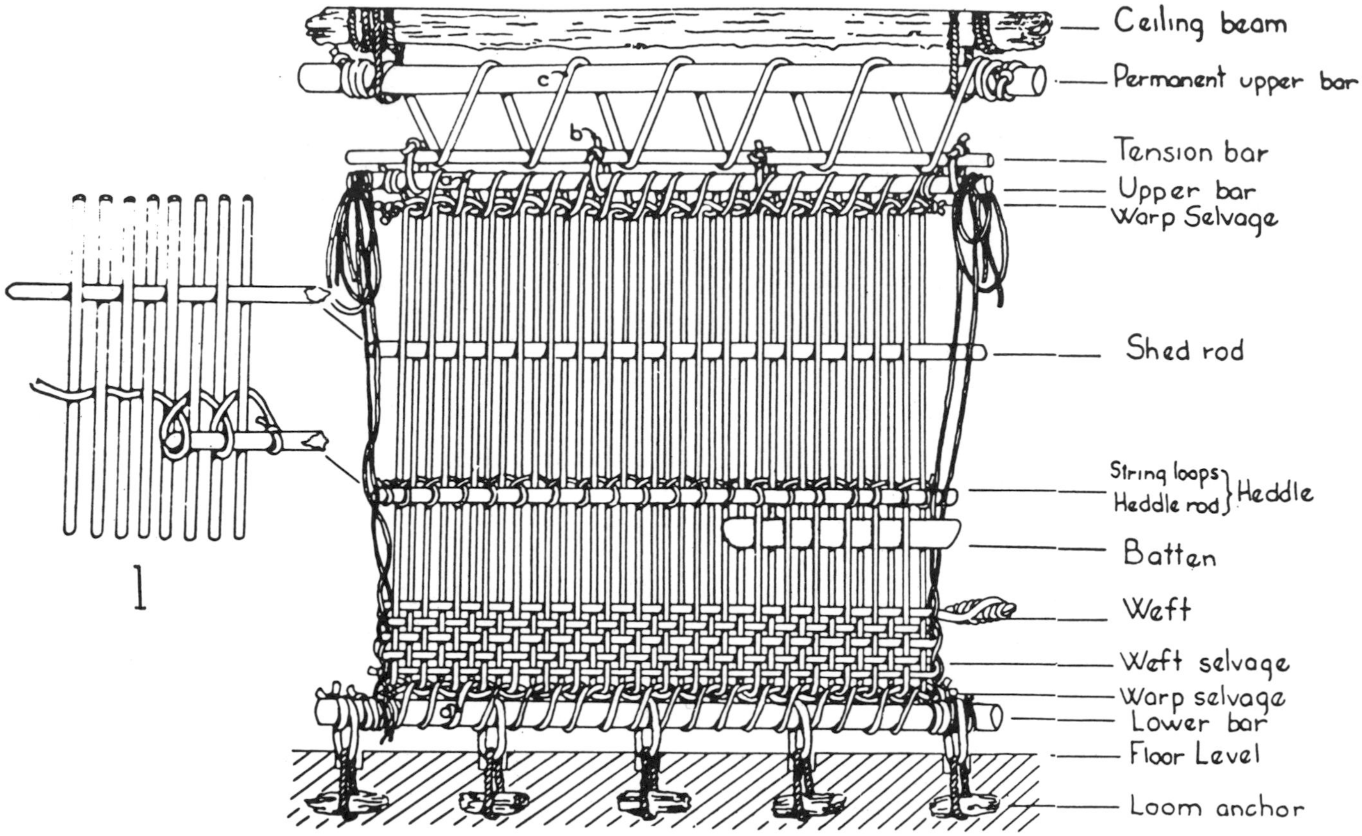

Ceiling beam
Permanent upper bar
Tension bar
Upper bar
Warp Selvage
Shed rod
String loops
Heddle rod
Heddle
Batten
Weft
Weft selvage
Warp selvage
Lower bar
Floor Level
Loom anchor

1

2

A

THE TRUE LOOM*

A. The vertical loom, rigged for plain weave. (1) Detail showing the rigging of string loops to the heddle rod. (2) A diagram of the loom and its working parts. (3 and 4) Diagrams illustrating the functions of shed rod and heddle in changing sheds. Only two warps, e and o, are drawn in. These represent, respectively, the even-numbered and odd-numbered warps. The shed rod passes behind e — or behind all the even numbered warps (2, 4, 6, 8, etc.) Heddle loops clasp o, or all odd-numbered warps. In diagram 3 the heddle is shown pulled forward, and the batten, b, inserted behind o and turned sideways to open the shed for the first weft, wl. In 4 the shed rod is shown forced down against the heddle loops, and the batten holding open the shed thus formed. The second weft, w2, is in position.

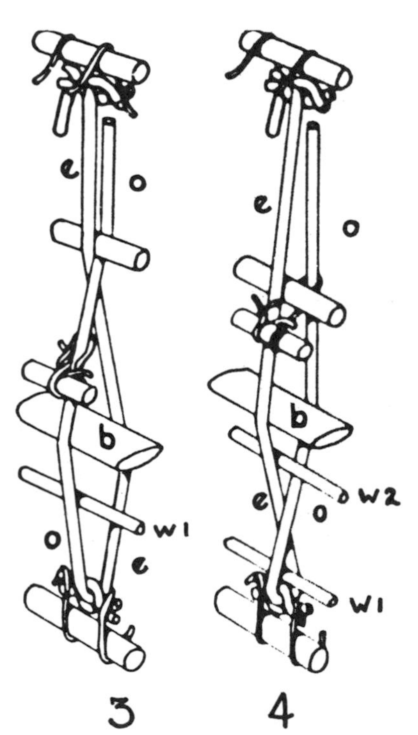

*Loom drawings by
Frances R. Raynolds and Malcolm Withers
November 1957 Page 42
Transactions of the American Philosophical Society.

Foreword

"The Story of Navaho Weaving" is the first of a series of scientific publications launched by the Heard Museum of Anthropology & Primitive Art. This booklet is the result of an intensive study and analysis made on the museum collection of Navaho textiles by Mrs. Kate Peck Kent.

Shortly after their arrival in Arizona in the 1890's, Mr. and Mrs. Dwight B. Heard started collecting a representative sample of the material culture of the many Indians of the Southwest. They were quick to perceive the inherent beauty and fine craftsmanship found in Navaho rugs and blankets woven at that time, and bent every effort to assemble a representative collection of the best rugs available. Today this valuable and important collection is housed in the Heard Museum, Phoenix, Arizona, and through this booklet we are happy to present information about this collection.

It is generally conceded among students and collectors that the publication of "Navaho Weaving" by Charles A. Amsden in 1934 gave American ethnology "the" definitive book about this subject. Unfortunately it was out of print for a number of years, and although it is now in the 2nd edition, it is not up to date. What has happened to the handicraft during the past quarter century is very important and relatively unstudied. Chapters IV and V of this brochure will supply some of the answers to questions so frequently asked by those who want to know the status of Navaho weaving today and to read an educated guess as to its future.

The controversial spelling of "Navaho" vs. "Navajo" may be simplified by saying that either is correct. The word "Navahu" is taken from Tewa speech (The Tewa are Pueblo tribes belonging to the Tanoan Linguistic family); in the 17th century the Spanish called them "Apaches de Navajo". The Navaho people themselves do not use the word but refer to themselves as "Dine" which means "people". However you choose to spell it, the pronunciation is still NAVAHO!

The Heard Museum collection of Navaho textiles numbers over 125 pieces. The bulk of these were woven during the past 80 years and offer to the student some very fine examples of the best of the old historic rugs.

Through the generosity of Mr. Read Mullan of Phoenix, Arizona, we have included four plates illustrating examples of Mr. Mullan's superlative collection of modern Navaho rugs. Mrs. Kent has made a complete analysis of the entire collection and this detailed information is available to qualified students and collectors on request. The purpose of this small book is to offer the prospective owner of a Navaho rug a brief, concise and authoritative guide about what to look for in a good rug and some very interesting facts about the history of this craft.

Mrs. Kate Peck Kent is a qualified authority on the history of native textiles of the Southwestern Indians. In 1954 she published on the recovered archaeological textiles of Montezuma Castle National Monument, Arizona. In 1957 the American Philosophical Society published "The Cultivation and Weaving of Cotton in the Prehistoric Southwestern United States". This scientific contribution by Kate Kent is considered to be one of the best definitive pieces of textile research ever written. Mrs. Kent is associated with the Department of Anthropology, University of Denver, Denver, Colorado.

H. Thomas Cain, Curator,
The Heard Museum of
Anthropology and Primitive Art,
Phoenix, Arizona

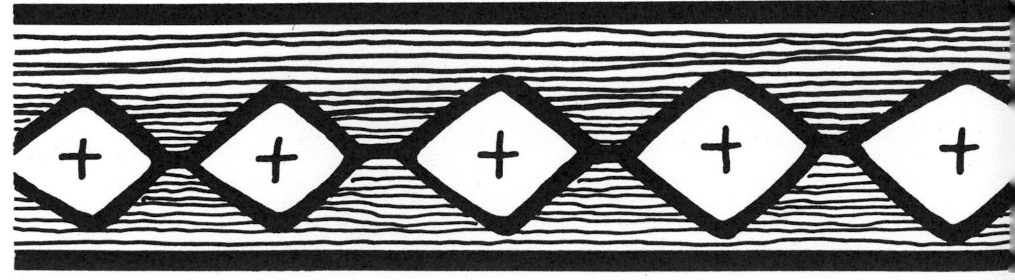

CHAPTER I

A Brief History of Navaho Weaving

The origin of weaving in the Southwest

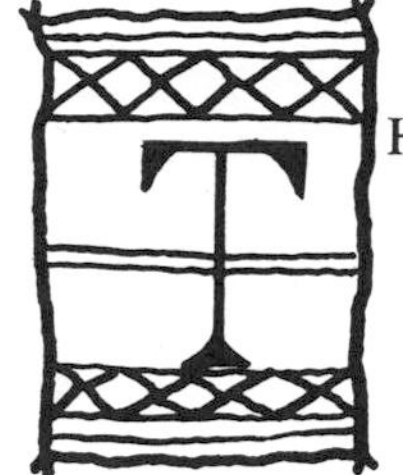

HE Spaniards, marching into the New Mexico Pueblos in 1540, found the people dressed in cotton clothing of excellent manufacture. The cloth was woven on a simple upright loom and handsomely patterned in geometric designs. The art of weaving cotton has since been shown by archaeologists to have been well established in the Southwest by 700 A.D.—possibly several centuries earlier than that in southern Arizona. The Spaniards valued Pueblo textiles highly, and the Rio Grande people were forced to supply their overlords with cotton blankets for export to Mexico and Spain. Benavides, writing in 1630, sets the annual tribute to the Spanish authorities as one "vara" (33 inches) of cotton cloth from every Pueblo household.[1] Subsequently, under the increasing pressures of white culture, the Puebloans shifted to European clothing and trade cloth, maintaining native costume only for ceremonial wear. At the present time no weaving (except for simple woolen belts for tourist sale) is done in the New Mexican Pueblos. A few men in the Hopi towns of northern Arizona still weave, concentrating their efforts on vegetable dye wool rugs and other articles for tourist sale rather than on the old traditional Pueblo cotton clothing.

The Navahos Learn to Weave, 1600-1700

By a curious set of circumstances, as this ancient American art diminished among the Pueblos, it became increasingly firmly established among the Navahos, whose name is now almost synonomous with "Indian rugs."

The chain of events by which the Navaho took over and developed weaving as one of their distinctive arts, forms the theme of this booklet. These people, relative newcomers into the Southwest by comparison with the Pueblos, were living principally in northwestern New Mexico in the sixteenth and seventeenth centuries. They farmed, hunted and raided the settled Pueblo and Spanish towns. There is no evidence of weaving among them prior to 1700. Before that date, however, they were building up large flocks of sheep. With an adequate supply of wool at hand, the stage was set for their weaving.

During the increasingly troubled years of the late sixteen hundreds, and particularly after the Pueblo Rebellion against the Spanish in 1680, Indian villagers from the Rio Grande moved in with the Navaho to avoid reprisals from the Spanish authorities. There was every opportunity for an exchange of ideas between Navaho and Pueblo, and it is highly probable that the Navaho learned to spin and weave the wool of their sheep at this time. Perhaps this occurred in the Gobernador area of northwest New Mexico, where one finds Pueblo ruins and Navaho hogan rings combined in a number of refugee sites.

In any event, from about 1700 on, there are references to Navaho weaving. That it was learned from the Pueblos, and not from Mexican settlers, is an indisputable fact. All the basic technical processes—spinning with shaft and whorl spindle; the upright loom with its simple heddle and shed rod for controlling warp sets; the waist loom for manufacturing narrow belts; the sword-like wooden batten for beating down wefts; the extra yarns twisted along warp and weft selvages — these features, as well as certain distinctive ideas of patterning, are quite definitely non-European. (Plate 1) The only technical innovation has been the use of commercial cards with metal teeth for combing fibers straight before spinning. The simple Pueblo loom,

1 Amsden, pp. 128-129

easily dismantled into nothing more than a set of sticks and poles, suited the semi-nomadic Navahos as the stationary European hand loom could never have done.

Traditional Navaho clothing, used to some extent almost until 1900, closely resembled Pueblo attire—a further indication of the original source of Navaho weaving. Men's and women's striped shoulder blankets, rectangles whose greater dimension runs with the wefts, are shaped exactly like the Pueblo "manta"—a blanket used as a wrap-around dress for women, or a shawl by men or women. (See page 9). The Navaho woman's blanket dress and the man's shirt were also based on Pueblo models.

Weaving Becomes an Important Navaho Craft, 1700-1850

In 1706 the Navaho are described as owning woven clothing. This may well have been of their own manufacture, although the point cannot be proved. By the late 1700's, however, the Navaho were well established as weavers, supplying blankets to other Indians and Spanish. In 1812 one writer states: "Navaho woolen fabrics are the most valuable in our province (New Mexico) and Sonora and Chihuahua (as well)."[2] The Navaho within 100 years had superseded their Pueblo teachers as the major source of native woven textiles in the Southwest, and had turned from wearing hide to woolen clothing. Of actual examples we have few prior to 1850. These are, with one exception, plain tapestry weave patterned by very narrow stripes of natural white, brown, and black wool, with the addition of limited amounts of native-dyed yellow, reddish brown and green, and some bayeta red and indigo blue. They take the form of fragments, gathered from Massacre Cave in Canyon del Muerto and White House in Canyon de Chelly. One piece from the former site, is a delicately woven twill patterned in indigo blue, black and white stripes. A complete brown and white striped blanket shaped like a Pueblo manta, from a burial in "Navaho country", also survives. All these are believed to date to the very early 1800's.

The evidence is scanty, but from it we judge that weaving became increasingly important among the Navaho from 1700-1850 and that fabrics throughout this time were patterned mainly in narrow stripes, a very simple way of working color into a textile.

Navaho Weaving from 1850 to the Present

Basic trends in Navaho weaving since 1850 are not so difficult to follow. We are no longer working with a few tantalizing bits of evidence, but with a considerable quantity of complete blankets and rugs. The changes that appear in these fabrics over the last 110 years or so can only be understood in terms of certain historical events in the lives of the people. These events established four major periods in weaving. The first three of these will be treated in detail in Chapter II, and the fourth in Chapters III and IV.

1. *The Classic Period, 1850-1875.* Throughout these years Navaho women concentrated their efforts, as in former times, on the weaving of various articles of clothing for their own families, plus blankets, both for themselves and for sale or trade to Mexicans, other Indians, and American soldiers. This was the period of greatest technical excellency in spinning and weaving — a proficiency lost in the subsequent period, and only recaptured in a few contemporary pieces.

Between the years 1863 and 1868 the Navaho people, rounded up by American soldiers under Kit Carson as punishment for their depredations on Mexican and Pueblo villages, were impounded in a reservation forty miles square, the Bosque Redondo, at Fort Sumner, in

2 Amsden, p. 133

east central New Mexico. With this tragic event, the traditions of the Classic Period began to disappear.

2. *The Transition Period, 1875-1890.* The years from 1875 to 1890 mark a period of change in Navaho weaving. This was essentially a transition from weaving for home consumption to becoming established in the tourist market. The people, returned to their homelands from Bosque Redondo, began again to build up their flocks. Classic traditions in weaving lingered for a time, but increasing contacts with whites brought important changes. By 1880 the railroad had pushed through to New Mexico and Arizona, opening the area to tourists and commercial trade goods. The number of traders to the Navaho multiplied rapidly in the early '80's. These men supplied the Indians with commercial weaving yarns and dyes. They also furnished yard goods and commercial clothing, thus doing away with the need for native-woven textiles. The quality of Navaho weaving degenerated and the craft might well have died out altogether at this time. It was saved from extinction through the demand for Indian blankets created by the tourist market — a market quickly exploited by enterprising traders and weavers. In answer to the needs of an alien culture, Navaho women turned from the weaving of clothing and blankets to the manufacture of floor rugs. This basic modification was completed by 1890.

3. *The Rug Period, 1890-1920.* Increased commercialization of the craft brought with it a further lowering of standards, in spite of the efforts of certain interested traders and dealers to encourage high quality work. A number of developments occurred during these years which are significant to an understanding of present-day weaving, but, with some exceptions, Navaho rugs had deteriorated markedly in technique and design by 1920.

4. *The Revival Period and Contemporary Weaving, 1920-1961.* The story of the revival of Navaho weaving deals with the various steps taken since 1920 to improve the quality of yarn, color, design and weave technique in Indian rugs. Perhaps the most dramatic incident concerns the renewal of interest, at least on the eastern part of the Reservation, in Classic and Transitional Period weft-stripe patterns, and the development of native vegetable dyes.

CHAPTER II

Important Types of Navaho Textiles From the Classic to the Revival Period

(1850 - 1920)

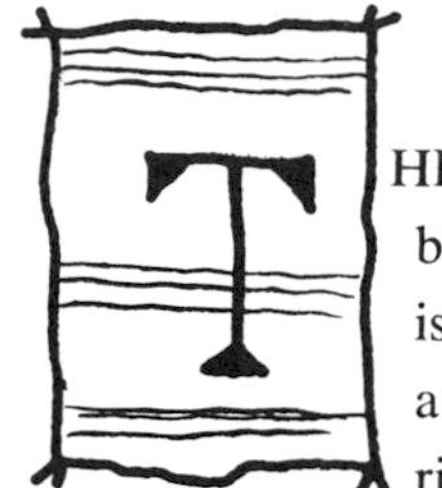

THE following discussion of important blanket types between 1850 and 1920 is necessarily brief. It can give only a limited idea of the tremendous variety actually to be found in Navaho weaving of these 70 years. The story is complicated by the fact that certain styles characteristic of one period — as the classic "chief" blanket, for example — might continue to be woven in modified form in successive periods, even to the present day. Our discussion of such a style necessarily carries us ahead of our story from time to time.

We have not the space necessary to discuss weave techniques in detail. This has been well done by Amsden and others.[3] All the blankets and rugs described were woven on the stationary upright loom. (Page 2) With the exception of twills (see page 26), all are plain weave tapestries. To accomplish this weave, alternate warps are attached by string loops to a slender stick called a *heddle,* which rests in front of the warps and horizontal to them. Pulling the heddle automatically brings forward the set of warps attached to it. A weft is drawn in behind this set. The remaining warps are forced forward for the next weft pick by a rod passed behind them. This rod is called the *shed rod.* Each weft pick is beaten down close on the one below with a sword-like stick called a *batten.* Warps are usually completely concealed by wefts.

The Classic Period, 1850-1875

The beginning date for this Period — 1850 — simply marks the year when records and actual examples of Navaho weaving became adequate for study. Actually, if we had loom products in quantity from the preceding years — at least as far back as 1800 — we should probably find the same kinds of yarn and dyes; the same excellence of spinning and weaving; the same types of woven articles, and the same emphasis on striped patterns that are so characteristic of the Classic Period. These years, in other words, mark the climax of well-established native traditions, which were soon to be so strongly modified by contacts with an alien culture.

Weave materials included handspun native wool yarn, threads raveled from bayeta and other commercial cloths, and Saxony yarn. *Handspun yarn* is made by twisting fibers into a single ply or strand. If intended for warps, this strand may be re-spun three or four times into a very thin, strong yarn. Less tightly spun yarn served as wefts. The bulk of Navaho weaving during the Classic Period and down to the present time has been done with native-spun yarns. Handspun was either used in natural colors — white, black or brown — or dyed in a limited number of colors. The most common dye was *indigo blue,* obtained through trade with the Spanish. Indigo, imported in the form of dry chunks from Mexico, had probably been used by the Navaho from the time they first learned to weave. Very few native dyes were in use at this time. The color of natural brown or black wool might be darkened and improved by use of a vegetable dye, and one finds some green and yellow tones. For the most part, however, the Navaho satisfied their desire for color by turning to trade materials.

Most important of these was *bayeta.* "Bayeta" is the Spanish name for a cloth of English manufacture —

3 See bibliography, page 46

baize — which was brought into the Southwest via Mexico and traded by the piece to the Indians. It was dyed in a number of colors, but, with very few exceptions, red was the Indians' choice. The cloth was laboriously raveled, and the single threads thus obtained employed as wefts. They were either loosely re-twisted by twos, threes, or fours, or simply used in pairs or threes without twisting. The soft red tones of bayeta were derived from a dye called "cochineal". Cochineal consists of the dried, crushed bodies of tiny insects found in the Canary Islands, Java, and Mexico. Bayeta threads frequently exhibit small white spots. These spots resulted from the cloth being dyed after weaving, the dye not always penetrating where warp and weft threads crossed. When the cloth was raveled, the undyed spots appeared. Tales of raveling the uniforms of soldiers killed in skirmishes with the Indians, while they add a certain romantic touch to the story of Navaho blankets, and while they cannot be disproved, should be regarded as little more than imaginative fiction. Cloth was readily available in large bolts.

Bayeta threads were used by the Navaho from at least the early 1800's until the end of the Classic Period. In the 1870's and '80's raveled threads of quite a different character came to be used. These were extracted from commercial American bed blankets, flannel cloth and red flannel underwear. The newer raveled threads can usually be distinguished from true bayeta by their garish aniline color, and by the fact that the fibers tend to have a matted surface appearance. Like bayeta, the threads often show small white specks.

Another commercial material found in Classic Period blankets is Saxony yarn. This yarn, manufactured in Germany, was imported into the Southwest by 1850 or earlier. It is generally three-ply, the plies having a tight, regular twist. Red is the color usually found, but a number of other shades do appear. Saxony yarns have a definite sheen when held up to the light. It has been suggested that this yarn may have been supplied by soldiers to Navaho women at Bosque Redondo, so that souvenir blankets could be woven. This is a reasonable supposition, as there would have been little native wool available at that time.[4] Saxony yarns will usually be found in small stripes or pattern details with bayeta and handspun. Blankets woven entirely of this material are rare.

Designs of the Classic Period lean heavily on simple weft stripes. During this time, however, other design ideas were being tried, probably inspired in part by patterns on blankets of Mexican manufacture. New designs include rectangles, crosses, zigzag horizontal lines and diamond-shaped figures. All the elements of these figures are based on the right angle, which produces terraced, or stepped, diagonals.

Types of textiles woven included men's shirts, women's dresses, saddle blankets, saddle cinches, belts, hair ties and wearing blankets of varying degrees of excellence. We shall consider here only three outstanding blanket types. One of these, taking its shape from the Pueblo manta, is the so-called "chief" blanket. The other two are shaped like the Mexican serape, the longer dimension running with the warps.

1. *Men's and Women's Shoulder Blankets, or "Chief" Blankets.* A direct copy of the Pueblo manta, the so-called "chief" blanket may be recognized by its oblong shape, the longer dimension running with the wefts. The average size of the man's shoulder blanket is about 50 inches with the warps, by 70 inches with the wefts. Women's blankets average 45 by 60 inches. The term "chief" has no particular significance, since these blankets never functioned as a symbol of rank.[5]

The earliest known complete example of Navaho weaving was of shoulder blanket proportions, and patterned in alternating brown and white weft stripes. (See page 6) Blankets of this type collected in the 1850's

4 Amsden, p. 183
5 Douglas, 1951, p. 50

show the center stripe widened markedly by comparison with the others, and also a tendency for the colored edge stripes to be somewhat broader. Stripes are black and white — natural wool colors. In a few cases red was substituted for black in the three broad center and edge stripes. (Plate 2) Interest was added to the somewhat monotonous pattern by introducing narrow lines of colored wefts, bars, and simple designs, into center and edge bands. One standard type of the early Classic Period shows narrow lines of indigo blue handspun employed in this fashion. In another, short parallel bars of red were placed at the center and both ends of all three bands so that there were nine prominent "spots" of color. Rectangles were sometimes substituted for simple color bars. (Plate 3).

The most characteristic "chief" blanket pattern was an elaboration of the nine-spot theme. It consisted of a diamond with terraced sides centered on the broad mid-band, quarter diamonds at the blanket corners, and half diamonds at the mid-points of the blanket edges. The centers of the diamonds might contain a variety of simple figures such as bars or crosses.

After a peak period from 1850-1880 the appearance and feel of shoulder blankets changed rapidly. Keeping the basic layout of the design, and the shape, weavers switched to manufacturing heavy floor rugs. The nine-spot pattern, in most cases, came to dominate the design, with stripes greatly reduced in importance. Diamond figures increased in size, sometimes meeting at their upper and lower tips, so that the main lines of the design ran vertically, or parallel to the warps, rather than horizontally. As in other Navaho textiles woven after 1880, terraced figures tended to be replaced by serrate, or diamond style figures. (Plate 4. See page 21).

Design development in women's shoulder blankets followed somewhat the same course. Tradition decreed, however, that the stripes inserted between broad edge and center bands be much narrower than those in the man's blanket, and that gray replace white. There was a marked tendency, too, to weave patterns running the full length of the three broad stripes, rather than to focus attention on nine distinct spots of color. (Plate 5).

Rugs patterned after shoulder blankets were in some demand throughout the early 1900's. Occasionally today a weaver produces a copy of a classic "chief" blanket.[6]

2. *Classic Period blankets of good manufacture.* During the 1850's and '60's hundreds of plain striped blankets called "dougies," woven of natural white, black, and brown coarse handspun wool yarns, were produced by the Navaho for their own use and for trade. We are not concerned here with these, but only with the superior grade of wearing blanket, featuring finely-spun yarns, bayeta, and Saxony. These may be placed in two classes on the basis of design. In blankets of the first class terraced figures were worked on a solid color background — usually red. (Plate 6) In the second, the background consisted of narrow stripes subordinated to the rest of the pattern. Sometimes the stripes were broken into short parallel bars by the main lines of the design. (Plate 7) Not infrequently the design resembled that of chief blankets of the same period, with the center band emphasized, and the four corners marked off by diagonal lines.

Classic Period design lingered on into the '80's, so that it is sometimes found on blankets woven of commercial aniline-dyed yarns.

3. *"Moki" pattern, or banded background blankets.* A second type of finely-woven serape-shaped wearing blanket, important in the Classic Period, is characterized by a pattern of very narrow alternating, black or brown and indigo blue weft stripes. The monotony of

6 The Heard Museum collection includes a rug recently collected at Bitahochee, Arizona, which copies a Classic Period "chief" blanket in red, blue, black, and white. The dyes are aniline.

PLATE 2. A handsome example of a man's shoulder blanket, with red substituted for the more usual black as the basic color in middle and edge bands. Inset in these bands are bars of indigo blue and green.

DATE. Circa 1880. SIZE. 51 by 63 inches. THREAD COUNT. 44 handspun, 54 raveled or commercial yarn wefts; 10-11 warps per inch. MATERIALS. WARP: Commercial cotton twine. WEFTS: white, brown, black—natural color handspun; pinks and reds—raveled threads, used singly or in pairs, aniline dye; blue—handspun, indigo dye; green—4-ply commercial yarn, aniline dye faded to yellowish-white.

PLATE 3. Man's shoulder blanket showing the use of small rectangles rather than sets of short parallel bars in edge and center panels.

DATE. 1875-1880. SIZE. 42 by 51 inches. THREAD COUNT. 46 wefts; 8 warps per inch. MATERIALS. WARP: handspun. WEFTS: white—handspun; brownish-black—handspun, natural wool color possibly darkened with native dye; green—handspun, native dye; blue—handspun, indigo dye; reds—raveled threads used singly, commercial aniline dye.

PLATE 4. "Chief" blanket of the Transition Period, probably made for sale as a rug. The nine-spot pattern has become enlarged, tending to dominate the stripes.

DATE. 1880-1890. SIZE. 50 by 63 inches. THREAD COUNT. 36-40 wefts; 8 warps per inch. MATERIALS. Handspun, commercial aniline dyes.

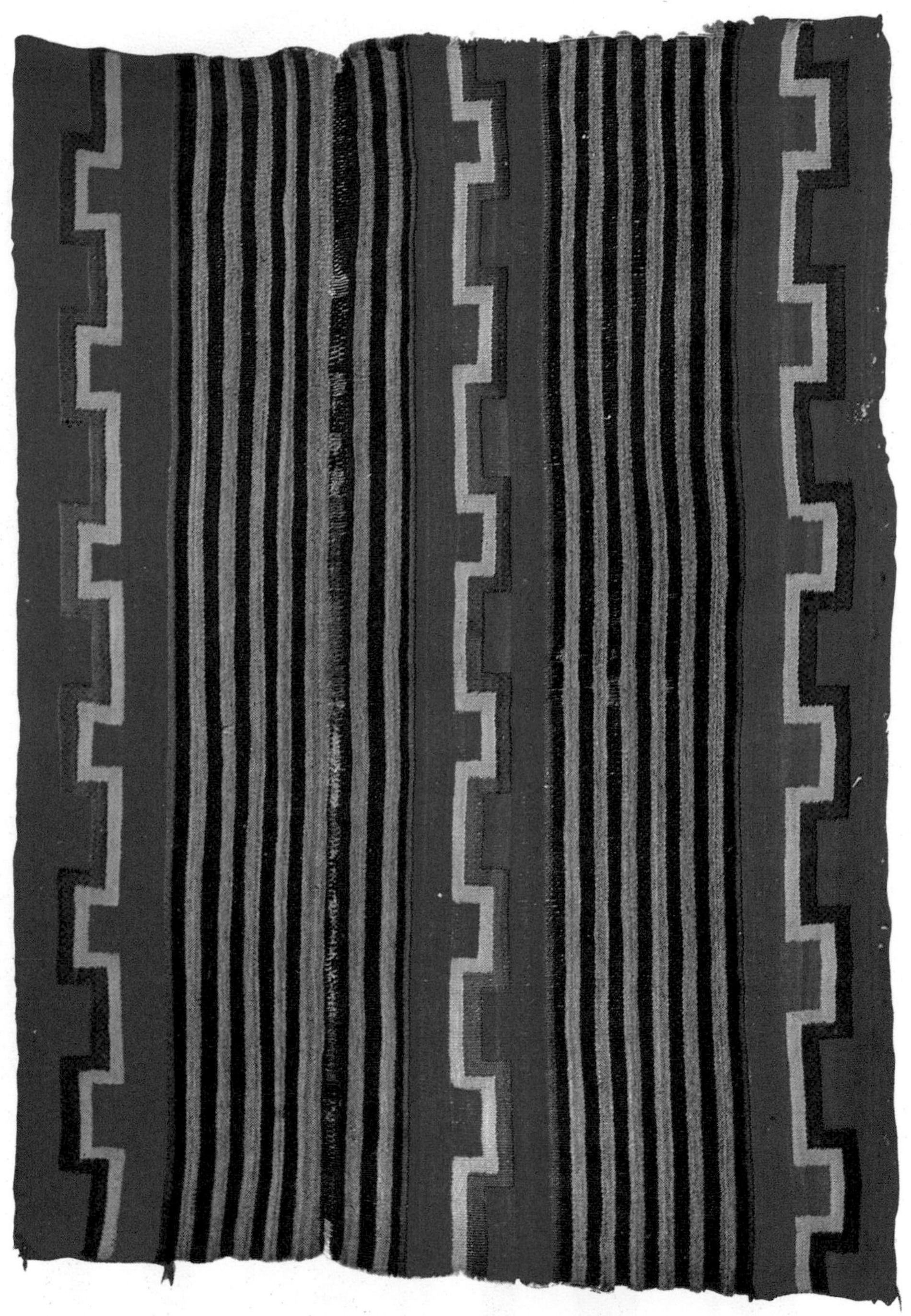

PLATE 5. Woman's shoulder blanket, showing the characteristic narrow gray and black striping and a continuous pattern in the three design bands.

DATE. 1880-1890. SIZE. 39 by 56 inches. THREAD COUNT. 20-24 wefts; 7-8 warps per inch. MATERIALS. All handspun. Red and green—commercial aniline dye. Blue—probably indigo. Black—dye, source unknown.

PLATE 6. A blanket of Classic Period terraced design against a solid color background. This was collected near Fort Apache, Arizona, where it was found tacked to an old wool comforter being used as an automobile seat cover. The end selvages have torn off, leaving warps extending so as to give the appearance of a fringe.

DATE. 1870-1875. SIZE. 50 by 58 inches. THREAD COUNT. 54 wefts; 11-13 warps per inch. MATERIALS. WARP: handspun. WEFTS: White—handspun; blue—handspun, indigo dye; red—raveled, pre-aniline dye.

PLATE 7. A late Classic Period blanket with broken-stripe background, woven principally of early Germantown 3-ply yarns. DATE. 1875-1880. SIZE. 44 by 68 inches. THREAD COUNT. 40-50 wefts; 12 warps per inch. MATERIALS. WARP: handspun wool. WEFTS: blue—4-ply commercial yarn, aniline dye; remainder—3-ply commercial yarn, aniline dye.

the design is relieved by the insertion of somewhat broader white weft stripes, and bands of "beading" in blue and white or black or brown and white. "Beading", in textile terminology, refers to the weaving of a narrow band in which tiny blocks of color alternate. This means of adding interest to a weft stripe was widely used in prehistoric Pueblo fabrics, carried over into historic times by Pueblo weavers, and taught to their Navaho pupils. (Plates 8 and 9).

The simplest, and probably earliest, form of Moki pattern blankets featured only the narrow stripes. Later, limited amounts of red, and sometimes other colors, were worked into conservative band designs, which alternate with zones of narrow striping. In the Classic Period terraced figures appear in the colored bands, and in the 1880's terraced or serrate patterns spread out over the surface of the blanket, the sober striping simply furnishing a dark unobtrusive background.

Dating Moki style blankets must be done on the basis of yarns, dyes, and design. The plain-striped blankets, containing handspun, natural color or indigo blue dyed yarns may date as early as the '50's, and probably were being woven well before that time. Those containing bayeta or Saxony, and terraced patterns probably date to the '60's or '70's. The use of serrate patterns, raveled flannel, aniline dyes or Germantown yarns marks a blanket as belonging to the Transition Period. Finally, there are floor rugs done in this style, but with commercial Germantown yarns. The indigo blue is replaced by a purplish aniline color. Terraced figures, generally in brilliant red and white, are superimposed on the banded background. These rugs represent a "revival" of the Moki pattern tradition which took place around Hubbell's Trading Post, Ganado, Arizona, in the 1890's. (Plate 10).

Moki pattern blankets were produced by the Pueblo Indians of Hopi, Acoma, and possibly other villages, in the mid-19th century, as well as by the Navaho. In the case of the blankets which are simply patterned with blue, black or brown, and white stripes, there is virtually no sure means of distinguishing Pueblo-made from Navaho-made examples.[7] For this reason, dealers formerly identified all such blankets as Pueblo-made, and called them "Moki" or "Moqui" blankets. This is the old name for the Hopi, and it is probable that the *principal* source of these blankets in the mid-1800's was the Hopi towns. The same style is found in Rio Grande Spanish colonial hand loom blankets made prior to 1870. These may, of course, be distinguished from Indian-made examples on the basis of technical features — principally the presence of a center "seam" and the absence of twisted selvage threads.

The Transition Period, 1875-1890

The use of indigo blue handspun, bayeta, and Saxony yarn diminished rapidly during the early years of the Transition Period. Threads raveled from commercial American goods were used for a time, but had largely disappeared by the early '80's. Aniline dyes, coarse handspun, and Germantown yarns became the standard materials.

Aniline dyes are derived from coal tar after a process discovered by W. H. Perkin, an English chemist, in 1856. The early anilines were harsh in tone, generally faded easily, and "ran" when wet. They were supplied to the Indians in small packets which also contained the necessary mordant. Simple to use, and highly varied in color, they quickly replaced indigo blue and vegetable dyes.

Commercial yarns of American manufacture — collectively called *"Germantown"* — were dyed with aniline. These yarns are generally 4-ply, although some examples of 3-ply Germantown yarn will be found

7 The presence of "lazy lines" is often taken as indicating Navaho manufacture. There is no proof, however, that Navaho women invariably wove in such a manner as to create these lines or that Pueblo men invariably did not.

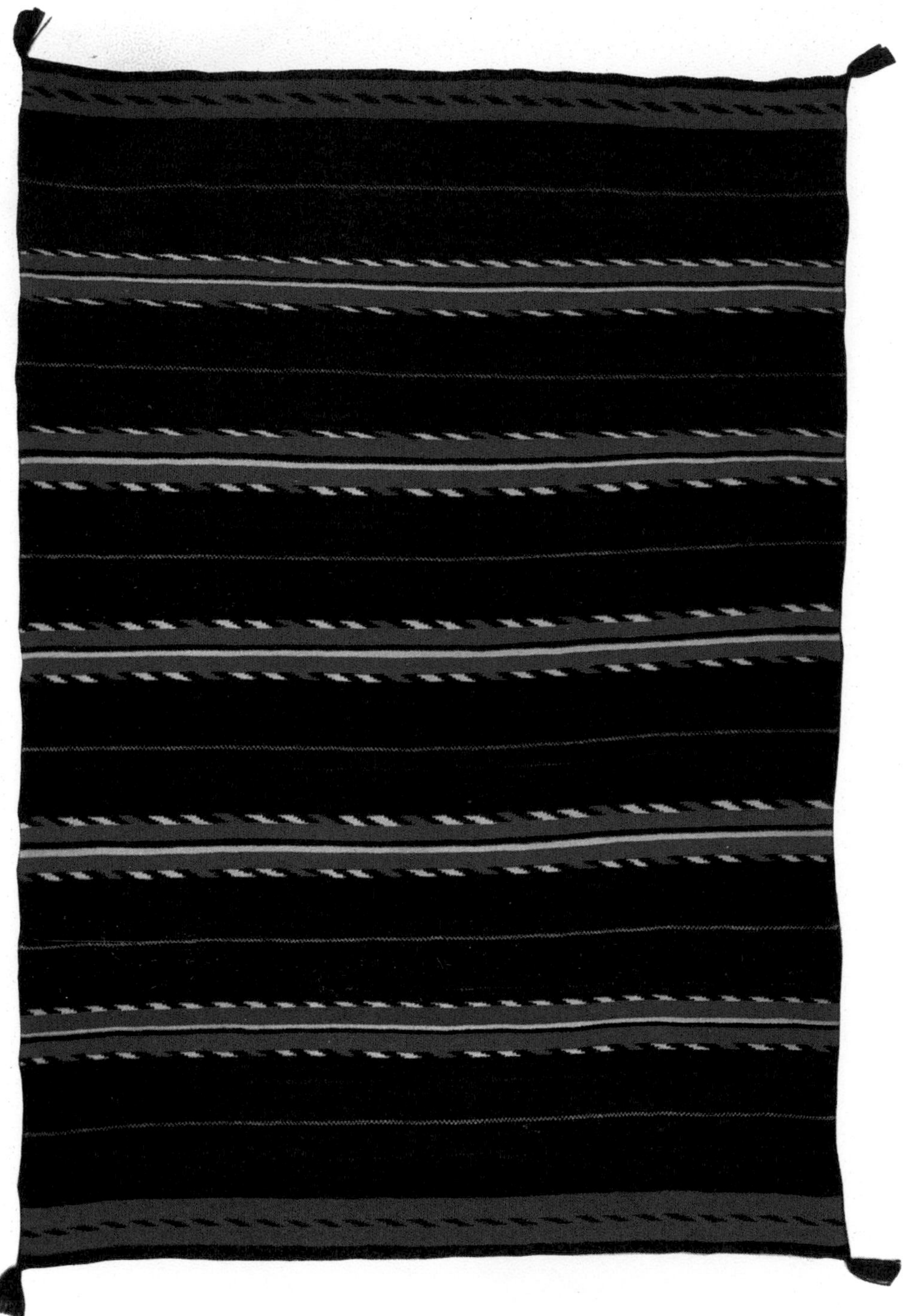

PLATE 8. "Moki" pattern blanket. Bands of red, narrow white lines, small stepped patterns in white, blue or red, and lines of beading in blue and white are set against the background of narrow blue and black stripes.

DATE. 1875-1880. SIZE. 47 by 69 inches. THREAD COUNT. 40 handspun, 50-54 raveled or commercial yarn wefts; 9-10 warps per inch. MATERIALS. WARP: handspun wool. WEFTS: white and black—handspun, natural color; blue—handspun, indigo dye; dark red—raveled threads plied in threes, probably aniline dye; light red—4-ply commercial yarn, aniline dye.

PLATE 9. A Transition Period "Moki" style blanket, the center diamond, woven in serrate style, shows the influence of Mexican textile patterns. Rows of beading in blue and white relieve the monotony of the striped background.

DATE. Circa 1880. SIZE. 53 by 76 inches. THREAD COUNT. 34 handspun, 44 commercial yarn wefts; 9-10 warps per inch. MATERIALS. WARP: handspun. WEFTS: white and brown—natural color handspun; blue—handspun, indigo dye; coral—4-ply commercial yarn, faded aniline dye.

PLATE 10. An excellent example of a late banded-background blanket woven as a result of the "revival" of this type at Hubbell's Trading Post, Ganado.

DATE. 1890-1900. SIZE. 49 by 71 inches. THREAD COUNT. 40-44 wefts; 10 warps per inch. MATERIALS. WARP: commercial cotton twine. WEFTS: 4-ply commercial yarn, aniline dyes.

in Navaho weaving of the early Transition Period. Three-ply Germantown may be distinguished from Saxony by its coarseness, by the fact that it lacks the sheen of Saxony, and by its harsh colors.

Cotton twine, another commercial product which was easy to get and simple to use, served as warps in many blankets of the Transition and early Rug Periods, although it never completely replaced hand-spun wool warps.

A new *design* idea arrived along with the adoption of commercial weave materials and dyes. This is the *serrate,* or *diamond,* style, which has dominated Navaho textile patterns from 1880 or '85 until now. Instead of basing her design on the right angle, which resulted in terraced, or stepped, lines and rectangular figures, the Navaho weaver introduced the acute angle, and produced smooth-edged oblique lines, and small triangular and diamond figures. This really involved a change in weave technique. The vertical lines of the rectangle parallel warps and are produced when two wefts of different colors meet and turn back through the warps. If these two wefts are not joined in some way, a slit, or hole, will eventually appear in the fabric between the two colored figures. Ordinarily this is avoided by the Navaho weaver, who loops the two wefts about each other between adjacent warps, or carries them around a common warp before weaving them back through the web. In weaving a diamond figure, however, the wefts, when they meet, are not usually interlocked. Tiny holes, one or two weft picks in size, are actually left in the cloth. These do not show, however, since they are offset along an oblique line — each succeeding hole a warp to right or left of its predecessor.

Even after diamonds replaced terraced elements, the traditional idea of arranging patterns in horizontal bands continued to be of primary importance. (Plates 11 and 12) There are an increasing number of examples in the Transition Period, however, in which the main lines of the design run the length of the piece, or vertically. (Plate 13)

In addition to diamond style patterns, a number of *pictorial* blankets were produced at this time. These bear realistic representations of birds, animals, men, houses, railroad cars, weaving combs, battens, or whatever else caught the imagination of the weaver. The earliest example of "figure-weaving" is believed to be that on a blanket taken from the body of an Indian at the Sand Creek Massacre in Colorado in 1864. This piece contains representations of four small ducks, which are almost obscured by the rest of the pattern — a conventional classic terraced composition. The making of pictorial blankets did not really become important, however, until 1880. Most examples were woven from aniline-dyed handspun wool or Germantown yarns. (Plate 14)

The figures are stylized and angular, in answer to the technical difficulties involved in executing them on the loom. For the most part, there is little attempt at composition. Figures are simply arranged in rows, or scattered almost at random over the blanket. Following this late 19th century tradition, a number of pictorial rugs are still being woven each year. These may feature houses, concha belts, a silhouette of Shiprock, or any number of other themes.

Pictorial blankets are in no sense ritualistic. The figures are not symbolic. They simply serve as decorative motifs. Somewhat different in nature are those rugs and blankets containing pictures of Navaho divinities, or *yeis.* These never serve a ceremonial purpose, being woven simply for sale to whites, but the figures have been copied from Navaho sacred sandpaintings. (Plate 15) Yei blankets were woven first around 1900 in the Farmington area in the face of strong tribal opposition.

PLATE 11. A Transition Period serrate pattern blanket or rug. The design is actually the old terraced stripe idea worked in diamond style.

DATE. 1880-1885. SIZE. 53 by 79 inches. THREAD COUNT. 28 wefts, 7 warps per inch. MATERIALS. All handspun, commercial aniline dyes.

PLATE 12. An extremely interesting example of the combination of design ideas and varied weave materials at the end of the Classic, beginning of the Transition, Period. The blanket shows a pattern of simple stripes, some beaded, on which is superimposed a diamond motif worked in serrate style. Bayeta and indigo appear in combination with 4-ply commercial yarn.

DATE. 1880. SIZE. 43 by 72 inches. THREAD COUNT. 44 wefts; 10 warps per inch. MATERIALS. WARP: handspun. WEFTS: white—handspun; blue—handspun, indigo dye; dark red—raveled bayeta, used in pairs or tripled, cochineal dye; green, yellow, coral—4-ply commercial yarn, aniline dye, faded.

PLATE 13. An early serrate pattern blanket, probably a child's shawl, with the main lines of the design running the length of the piece. (The weft edges have been repaired by overcasting with commercial red yarn.)

DATE. Circa 1880. SIZE. 31 by 47 inches. THREAD COUNT. 44-48 wefts; 11-13 warps per inch. MATERIALS. WARP: Handspun. WEFTS: white—handspun; blue—handspun in center third of blanket, shiny paired blue threads which appear to have been raveled from cloth at both ends, indigo dye; dark red—raveled bayeta, used in pairs or tripled, cochineal dye; light reds—some single-ply raveled and some 2-ply commercial yarn (probably a recent repair), aniline dye.

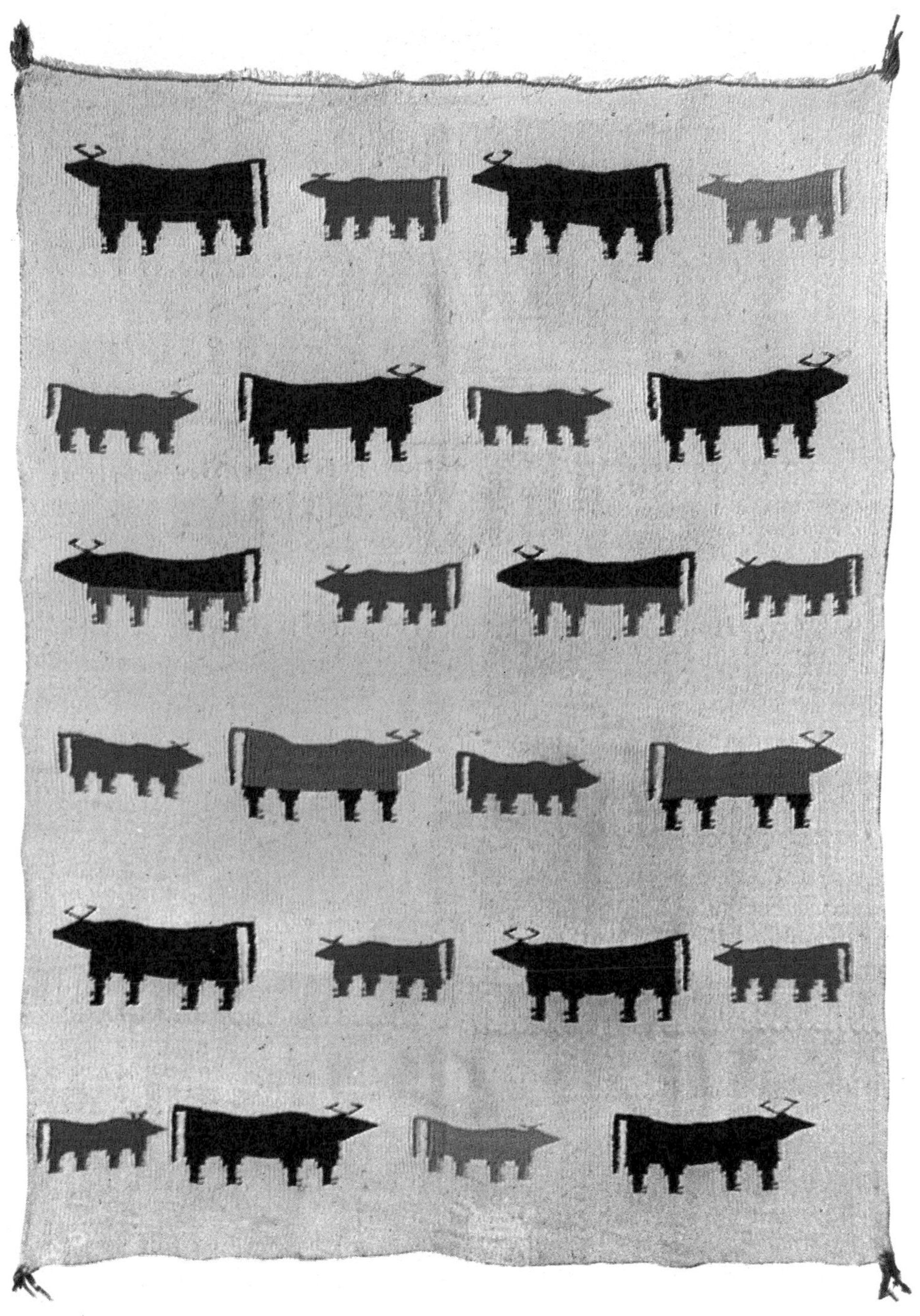

PLATE 14. A charming blanket with red, gray, black and green cows on a white ground. This type of pictorial blanket is sometimes called a "burial blanket", but had, in fact, no known connection with any funeral rites. (Mera, n.d., pp. 32-33)

DATE. Circa 1880. SIZE. 55 by 74 inches. THREAD COUNT. 28 wefts; 7 warps per inch. MATERIALS. WARP: handspun and some commercial 2-ply white yarn. WEFTS: handspun. Red and green —aniline dye; black and gray—probably natural color wool.

They are still produced there, and in the Lukachukai Mountains to the west. Less common are rugs, woven since the '30's in very limited numbers, on which replicas of whole sandpaintings appear. Only two or three women now do this work. Such blankets are expensive, retailing for around $700, and have become collectors' items.

Wedge-weave, or "pulled warp", a novel technical experiment by which oblique weft stripes were woven, became popular towards the end of the Transition Period and survived into the early 1890's. In this weave wefts are battened down so that they lie at an angle to the lower warp selvage, instead of parallel to it. This pulls the warp out of its normally vertical position. The warp slants first left, then right, in accordance with the angle at which weft picks are battened. The weft wedges of a wedge-weave are "scalloped" following the slant of the warps. Sometimes an entire blanket was woven in this technique while in other cases bands of wedge-weave alternate with bands of simple tapestry weave in which warps rest in their normal vertical position. (Plate 16) Wedge-weave blankets are usually woven of coarse handspun yarn, aniline dyed. A few examples contain Germantown yarn.

The Rug Period, 1890-1920

By 1890 the transition from weaving for home consumption to weaving almost solely for the tourist market had been accomplished. The standard material used at this time and throughout the Rug Period was coarse handspun wool, aniline dyed or natural color. Cotton warp and Germantown yarn wefts, fairly common in the 1890's, were frowned on by most traders, and had almost completely disappeared by 1900. Germantown did not bow out, however, without leaving its mark in the form of a distinctive type of design known as the *outline style.* Especially popular around 1890, this apparently represented an attempt by weavers to incorporate in a single blanket as many colors as possible. Each little diamond figure and oblique line was edged with a narrow row of contrasting color. The effect is usually dizzying (Plate 17), but many outline rugs are technically superior due to the fine, regular quality of the commercial weftage. With the passing of Germantown yarns, the outline style decreased in importance. It lingered on, however, principally in the region around Tees nos pas, west of Shiprock, where outline blankets, woven from handspun wool, are still made at the present time.

Late in the Transition, and in the early years of the Rug Period, a number of *twill weave* rugs and saddle blankets began to appear. A twill weave is one in which wefts float over selected sets of warps, rather than over and under alternate warps, as in regular plain weave. By this technique diagonal ribs of weft floats are produced. These form patterns of diamonds or vertical or horizontal zigzags, in accordance with the arrangement of warp sets. In setting up a loom for twill, the shed rod and two or more heddles are used, rather than just the shed rod and one heddle, as in plain weave. (See page 8) The number of heddles increases in accordance with the complexity of the design.

A variety of twills were produced by the prehistoric Pueblo weavers of the Southwest, and the art of twilling was passed on by them to the historic Pueblo and Navaho. One of the Massacre Cave fragments, presumably of Navaho manufacture, is a twill. Twilling was not, however, practiced by the Navaho to any great extent until the 1880's, and most examples date to the turn of the century. Twilling produces a thick, sturdy fabric, and is still used in making small floor rugs and saddle blankets. It is currently called "double cloth" or "double weave" by traders and dealers. (Plate 18)

As the rug business got well underway, conscious efforts were made by certain traders to stem the mounting tide of mediocrity and encourage the women to improve the quality, and hence the salability, of their products. J. Lorenzo Hubbell at Ganado encouraged the weaving of "Moki" style rugs. (See page 17) He also made a specialty of having very large floor coverings woven to order for American homes. Other attempts to encourage high quality rugs were made by the Fred Harvey Company and the Hyde Exploring Expedition. Cotton warp and Germantown yarn and also purple and green aniline dyes came to be banned. Only the best products of the loom were purchased for re-sale.[8]

Perhaps the most significant influence on weaving during this Period was that of J. B. Moore, who established a trading post at Crystal, New Mexico, west of the Chuska Mountains, in 1897. Moore sent wool east to be washed and carded. The thoroughly cleaned wool could be more evenly spun, and the technical quality of rugs woven in his vicinity thus began to improve. In addition to this, Moore, probably with the help of an artist friend, invented a new design style combining some traditional Navaho figures with other non-Navaho geometric motifs such as swastikas and frets. His patterns were enclosed by borders — either solid or figured. With the exception of some red, bright colors were discarded in favor of black, gray, brown, tan and white. These were natural wool tones — the grays and tans being made by combing white and dark fibers together before spinning. The Crystal tradition influenced Navaho weaving in two ways. It led, for one thing, to the distinctive style presently known as "Two Gray Hills", for the name of the trading post on the east side of the Chuskas south of Shiprock, where the style centers. (Plate 21 and 22) Here the old Crystal designs became increasingly elaborated, red was discarded entirely, and the technical excellence of spinning and weaving improved, until at present the best of the Two Gray Hills blankets are technically superior even to the finest Classic examples. Secondly, the idea of borders, the use of natural-color black, gray, brown and white yarns in combination with red, and the early Crystal patterns, spread throughout the Navaho Reservation by 1910. Much of the weaving today, especially in the western and northwestern parts of the Reservation, follows this early 20th-century style.

Around 1910 the United States Government, hoping to improve the meat-producing quality of Navaho flocks, introduced large numbers of Rambouillet sheep. These had oily, short-staple, crimpy wool, rather than the long-staple wavy wool of Navaho sheep. The new wool was difficult to clean, card and spin. Rugs woven from it were coarse; the white had a dirty gray cast; reds were dull. This, added to the stereotyped designs and the lack of good color, brought weaving to an all-time low. By 1920 the demand for Navaho rugs had fallen sharply, and those that found a sale commanded low prices.

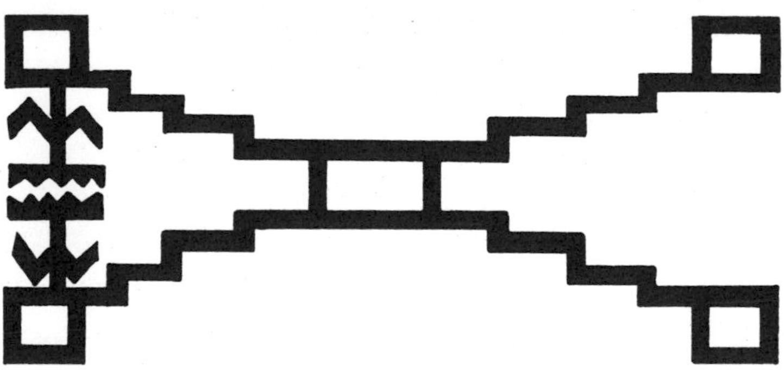

8 Amsden, pp. 193-194

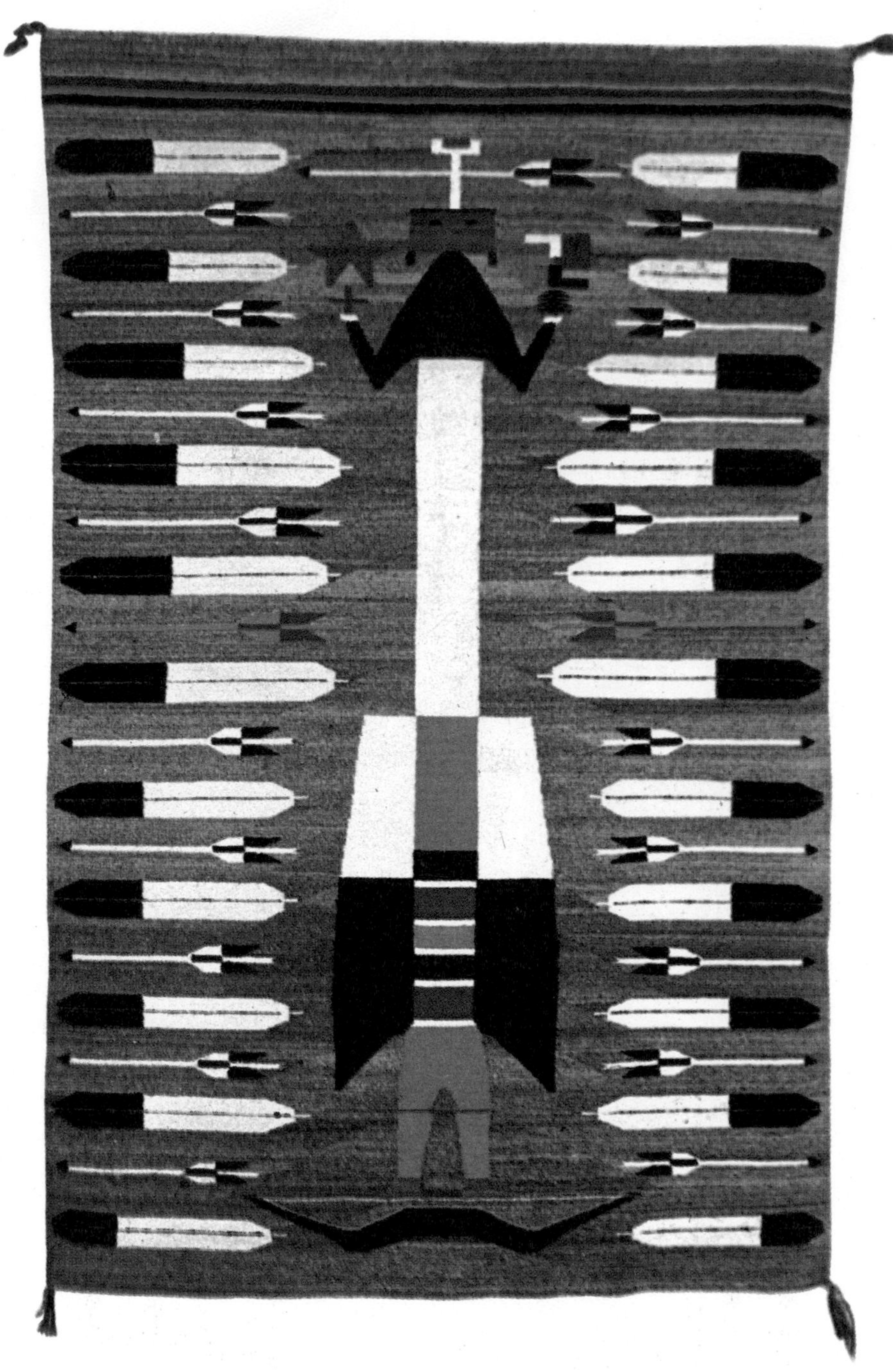

PLATE 15. Yei blanket, probably woven around 1910 in the Farmington area. SIZE. 40 by 63½ inches. THREAD COUNT. 42 wefts; 10 warps per inch. MATERIALS. WARP: commercial cotton twine. WEFTS: all handspun, aniline dye. Gray background probably made by spinning aniline-dyed black with white wool.

PLATE 16. A wedge-weave or pulled-warp rug. Bands of wedge-weave, showing characteristic oblique stripe pattern, and bands of ordinary plain weave tapestry, alternate.

DATE. 1880-1890. SIZE. 50 by 74 inches. THREAD COUNT. 20 wefts; 4-5 warps per inch. MATERIALS. All handspun, aniline dyes.

PLATE 17. A fine example of the serrate, or diamond, style with the main lines of the design running vertically, and the serrate figures edged by narrow lines of contrasting color. Warp ends are fringed by looping in short lengths of colored yarn.

DATE. Early 1890's. SIZE. 57 by 77½ inches. THREAD COUNT. 34-38 wefts; 11-12 warps per inch. MATERIALS. WARP: commercial cotton twine. WEFTS: commercial 4-ply yarn, aniline dyes.

PLATE 18. Diamond twill weave double saddle blanket, the two halves woven in different patterns.

DATE. Circa 1900. SIZE. 30 by 52 inches. MATERIALS. All handspun, natural color white and gray; aniline red.

CHAPTER III

The Revival of 1920

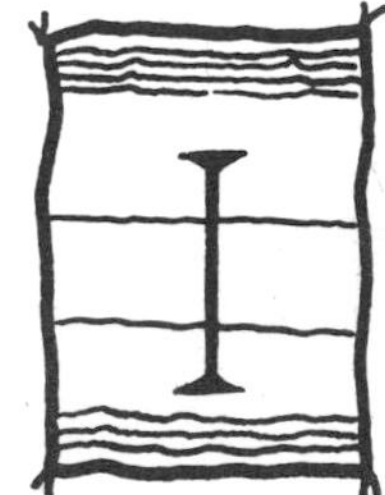

N the 1920's and '30's a number of people and groups became interested in improving Navaho weaving with a view to making the rugs again attractive to buyers. The first step was taken by Miss Mary C. Wheelwright of Boston, with the cooperation of Mr. L. H. McSparron of Chinle Trading Post. These two succeeded in persuading local Navaho women to experiment with vegetable dyes made from native plants. Miss Wheelwright also supplied the Indian women with sketches of designs taken largely from Transition Period blankets. The Eastern Association on Indian Affairs carried on her work in the early '30's. This organization interested the DuPont Company in manufacturing a series of chemical dyes in a wide range of pleasing shades especially designed for Navaho use. These proved too complicated for local conditions, as colorant and mordant had to be handled separately. Finally the makers of Diamond Dyes created a set of single-package dyes called *Old Navaho* which, although anilines, were more delicate in tone than the garish colors of the earlier commercial dyes.

Early Revival type blankets and rugs are characterized by soft, thick wefts, the extensive use of white, simple geometric patterns arranged in horizontal bands, and the lack of borders. Colors are either vegetable dye or soft anilines. In some of the first blankets of this type woven the pattern is very sparse and poorly conceived, as though representing timid and fumbling attempts to work with unfamiliar ideas.

Experiments with vegetable dyeing did not end with the Chinle venture, but were carried on in the mid-30's by the Home Economics Department of the Wingate Vocational High School.[9] They were strongly encouraged and backed also by Mr. and Mrs. William Lippincott of Wide Ruin Trading Post in the late '30's and '40's. It is largely as a result of the efforts of these two people that vegetable dye rugs in a number of soft pastel colors, and of superior manufacture, are the major loom products of the eastern part of the Reservation around Window Rock. Interestingly enough, there is no evidence that most of the vegetable dyes used today were known to Indians in earlier times. In other words, while the designs "revived" by Miss Wheelwright and others are definitely old Navaho, all but a very few of the dyes are recent discoveries made as the result of experimenting with whatever plant material seemed to offer possibilities for color.

Other moves aimed at protecting and improving Navaho rugs were made in the 1930's. The United States Government established a sheep farm at Fort Wingate for the purpose of developing a breed of sheep which would produce both good meat and high-grade, spinnable wool. Their efforts met with great success in producing a desirable breed. Uunfortunately, the experiment has not brought about any great improvement of Navaho flocks, nor has it made wool from its own sheep available over a great part of the Reservation.

In 1941 the Government also established the Navaho Guild as an agency for helping women to procure good wool and dyes, and to market their products. The Guild lapsed during World War II, but is presently operating at Window Rock, where it has been instrumental in encouraging excellent weaving, principally among the local women.

9 Bryan and Young, 1940

CHAPTER IV

Contemporary Navaho Weaving

THE current picture of Navaho weaving may be presented, very briefly, in terms of several important style centers.

Wide Ruin and Pine Springs at the southeastern edge of the Reservation in Arizona are well known for rugs of the borderless Revival style. These are woven in both natural-color and vegetable-dyed, handspun yarns of soft pastel. (Plate 19.)

Nazlini and Chinle weavers follow the same general style, but sometimes combine anilines with the vegetable dyes.

Crystal rugs tend to emphasize dark vegetable dyes—black, green, tan, yellow and rust. In recent years a specialty here has been the weaving of narrow "wavy" lines—a pattern created by alternating two or three weft picks of contrasting colors. The wavy line idea is currently spreading from Crystal to Wide Ruin and Chinle. (Plate 20.)

Two Gray Hills. Following the tradition established here around 1910, the weavers use natural brown, black, and white wools, carding some to make grays and tans. (Actually, the black is now intensified by dyeing.) Occasionally a bit of native-dyed yellow is used, and sometimes a little turquoise blue—the latter a commercial color. Designs are highly complex geometric compositions enclosed within solid or figured borders. The best of the Two Gray Hills, woven of exceptionally fine-spun yarn, are soft and thin, bearing more resemblance to blankets than floor coverings. Top-quality pieces command as much as $2200 retail. (Plates 21 and 22)

The *Shiprock* district has for many years been the principal source of yei blankets. Traditionally the figures are placed on a white background. Borders may or may not be present. Probably ninety percent of the yeis employ commercial yarn. Some are frankly tourist novelties, about three feet long, fringed along the warp selvages and selling for $7.00 or less.

Lukachukai and Upper Greasewood are now a second source for yei blankets. Usually the backgrounds are dark gray or tan, however, and the figures may be so stylized as to have a "streamlined" appearance. Yarns are either commercial or aniline dyed handspun. Coarse aniline rugs and some following the old-style standard red, black, gray and white bordered type of the early 20th century are also made here.

Tees nos pas Trading Post in the northeastern corner of Arizona, is the contemporary home of the 1890 outline style. (Plate 23. See page 26.) Other geometric pattern rugs are woven here also. Aniline dyes are the rule, and commercial yarn is being used in increasingly large amounts. Currently, a large (9′ by 12′) well-woven Tees nos pas rug may retail for as much as $1200.

Ganado and the region south to Klagetoh and southwest to Bitahochee and Indian Wells has been, until recently, a center for the production of red, black, gray and white rugs. Much of the red has a characteristic dark cast, and is known as "Ganado red". (Plate 24) As the result of influence from Wide Ruin, Pine Springs and Window Rock, the women are currently turning from this old style to the weaving of borderless, vegetable dye rugs.

As one moves west and northwest on the Reservation, the influence of the Revival on dyes and design almost disappears.[10] The bordered style of the early 1900's in black, white, brown, gray and red is with a few exceptions, the rule. Most of the local wool is poor for weaving. The white often has a grayish tone because of

10 Bartlett

PLATE 19. Contemporary Wide Ruin vegetable dye rug woven by Lottie Thompson. An interesting piece because it contains certain characteristic techniques and designs found in old Navaho blankets. The black and white vertically "striped" lines are made by alternating white and black weft picks. The "twisted" stripes of white and gray and pink and gray, which simulate twill, are found in many old blankets, sometimes actually being worked in twill technique. The comb-like edges of white and brown diamond figures appear first in blankets woven around 1890. The design probably originated with pictorial blankets which contained representations of the wooden comb used by weavers to force wefts down between warps. SIZE. 50 by 82 inches. THREAD COUNT. 44 wefts; 8 warps per inch. MATERIALS. All handspun. Gray—natural black and white carded together; other colors—vegetable dyes.

PLATE 20. A Crystal rug woven recently by Helen Peshlakai, Crystal Springs, New Mexico, and exhibiting the characteristic wavy-line pattern.

SIZE. 60 by 73 inches. THREAD COUNT. 20 wefts; 5 warps per inch. MATERIALS. All handspun, vegetable dyes.

PLATE 21. Somewhat less complex in design than contemporary examples, a handsome Two Gray Hills rug probably woven around 1930. The eight-pointed star may be derived from a type of New Mexican blanket called a "Vallero" and woven around 1890 in certain valleys of northern New Mexico (Mera, 1949, pp. 95-98).

DATE. Circa 1930. SIZE. 55 by 83½ inches. THREAD COUNT. 38 wefts; 9 warps per inch. MATERIALS. All handspun, natural color wools. Light tan background may be aniline dyed.

PLATE 22. Technically superior in quality, a contemporary Two Gray Hills rug woven by Anna Nez. Size 48 by 68 inches. THREAD COUNT. 52 wefts; 17 warps per inch. MATERIALS. All handspun wool. Black and brown darkened by dye, probably aniline. Gray-black carded with white; beige-brown carded with white.

PLATE 23. A contemporary Tees nos pas rug combining a complex geometric design of Two Gray Hills type with the use of bright colors and the idea of outlining characteristic of the 1890's.

SIZE. 54 by 103 inches. THREAD COUNT. 26-30 wefts; 9 warps per inch. MATERIALS. All handspun wool except for bright green wefts, which are 4-ply commercial yarn. Aniline dyes.

PLATE 24. A rug collected at Klagetoh in March, 1960 and woven by Mary Chee. It exemplifies the contemporary black-white-gray-aniline red, geometric patterned, bordered rug characteristic over most of the western part of the Reservation. The red is of the dark tone known as "Ganado red".

SIZE. 47 by 69½ inches. MATERIALS. All handspun wool. Red—aniline dye; black—probably natural color darkened with aniline dye.

improper washing. Cotton string has been used for warp to some extent since the last war, and handspun wefts are beginning to appear dyed in brilliant aniline colors as in pre-1900 days. Brightly colored commercial yarns will be found in a small number of rugs. The general quality of weaving in the west is inferior to that of Wide Ruin, Chinle, Pine Springs, Crystal and Two Gray Hills. However, there are some traders who encourage the women in their vicinity to weave fine rugs. Some significant style centers may be added to the eight already noted above.

Tuba City has been the center (though by no means the only source) since 1920 or before for the weaving of "storm pattern" rugs in black, white, gray and red. This pattern is said to have been copied from shipping tags on flour sacks sent to traders on the western part of the Reservation from Flagstaff by the Babbitt Company. It appears, however, to have originated with J. B. Moore at Crystal, New Mexico. Moore published a catalogue of rugs in 1911, which includes one bearing this design.[11] The storm pattern is allegedly symbolic, although the symbolism appears to be the white man's version of what an Indian should devise. Basic features of the pattern include: a center box, or square, which is variously called a "hogan", or "storm house", or "center of the world"; smaller boxes at or near each corner of the rug, called "houses of the wind"; four zigzag lines representing lightning, which connect the corners of the center square to each smaller box; two beetle-like figures, called "water bugs" or "pinyon beetles" at center top and bottom of the rug.

Coppermine, northwest of Tuba City, and *Chilchinbito,* twenty miles south of Kayenta, are the two centers on the western half of the Reservation where the best weaving is done. The district surrounding the latter post probably boasts the largest concentration of weavers on the Reservation. Some native dyes are used here.

From *Shonto and Inscription House north to Paiute Mesa and Navaho Mountain* the most typical rugs of the last ten or fifteen years have been woven in white, black, gray and native yellow dye. Unlike the true Revival style, the design is enclosed by borders.

Keams Canyon, in addition to the usual run of red, black, gray and white rugs, is at present handling some very large rugs (10′ to 15′ by 15′ to 30′ in size), some of which may sell for $2000 to $2400. These are a specialty of the weavers around Pinyon to the north of Keams Canyon.

Coal Mine Mesa near Tuba City is the center of a very recent experiment in improving weaving quality. High-grade wool has been supplied to the women, and they have been encouraged to revive older techniques and designs. Some excellent twills (double weaves) were turned out in 1960 as the result of these efforts.

This picture of weaving centers is not static. It will change from year to year as old ideas are exchanged between weavers of different districts, or new ideas developed by creative individuals. It should be remarked that double weaves come from many parts of the Reservation, but are produced in very limited numbers by comparison with the ordinary plain weave tapestry rugs which we have been discussing. One further point—nearly all trading posts handle small aniline-dye blankets of two types, the single saddle blanket and the double saddle blanket. These are of standard sizes—30" by 30" and 30" by 60". They are generally of coarse weave and poor design. In addition to the weaving centers mentioned, some saddle blankets and rugs, generally poor to mediocre in quality and woven of natural-color and aniline-dyed handspun yarns, are produced in the southwestern part of the Reservation and by weavers who set up shop along Highway 66 between Sanders and the Arizona-New Mexico line.

11 James pictures a storm pattern rug woven for J. A. Molohon and Company, Moore's successors. (Figure 203.) Occasionally a Two Gray Hills rug shows the main features of this pattern (See Mera, n.d., Plate 84).

CHAPTER V

What to Look For in a Navaho Rug And the Future of Navaho Weaving

THE discriminating buyer will find a variety of well-woven rugs available to him in craft shops in many cities and towns of the Southwest, and at Window Rock and most trading posts on the Reservation. The quality and variety of rugs is vastly superior to that of the pre-Revival Period. The choice of a textile will be governed first and foremost by the buyer's taste in color and design, by the amount he wishes to invest, and by the way in which he intends to use the rug. No one can dictate what these factors may be. However, the following points must be kept in mind if one intends to purchase a rug of good quality.[12] Edges should be straight and parallel. The corners of the rug should lie flat when it is extended full-length on the floor, and the rug itself should not wrinkle or bulge any place. Yarns should be evenly spun and battened down uniformly. Colors should be well matched. The warp must be wool, if the rug is to withstand any wear and tear. The buyer should ascertain the type of dyes used, and whether commercial yarn is present. (Aniline dyes and commercial yarns cannot be guaranteed against fading.)

There is rather general agreement on the part of traders and dealers that the demand for Navaho rugs, especially those which sell for $100 and under, is increasing. The problem for most dealers does not lie in selling rugs, but in getting enough to meet the rising demand. Vegetable-dye rugs, Two Gray Hills, yeis, and coarse anilines sell about equally well. Many people mistakenly consider vegetable-dye rugs to be "non-Indian" in character and won't buy them. An equally large number of buyers prefer vegetable dyes because the neutral colors fit the decor of modern homes. Yei blankets find a ready sale because of their pictorial quality, many being sold for wall-hangings.

A growing market does not mean that the future of Navaho weaving is assured. In spite of the fact that women can get two or three times as much as they did ten years ago for a given size rug, fewer weavers every year are producing rugs. Young women are not learning the craft; instead they are forsaking the loom for other careers, many becoming nurses, teachers, or secretaries. The reason lies in economics. The hourly wage earned by the average weaver is estimated to be between fifteen and twenty-five cents. Spinning, dyeing and weaving are physically hard, time-consuming tasks. When other more lucrative ways of earning money present themselves, the women quite naturally are attracted to them. The Navaho Tribal Council is currently developing various projects on the Reservation that will employ its people in less-exacting, financially more-rewarding, pursuits. In view of these facts, authorities connected with Navaho weaving doubt that the craft will survive to any great extent much longer. It is felt the native loom will fade into the past as did the spinning wheel of the Colonial settlers. There is disagreement as to how long this may take, but many feel it will occur within the next twenty years.

There are a few "name" weavers at the present time, women whose work is technically so superior that they can command a very high price for each rug. These individuals may continue to weave, as for them the pursuit is financially rewarding. Also, there are still some remote parts of the Reservation where alternative employment may not for a while be offered. One might find weaving continuing longer in those places. As paved roads, swift transportation, education, technocracy, business opportunity and modern tempo inevitably move across the Reservation, Navaho rugs will probably become the product of a few artisans only, and no longer a factor of economic importance in the life of the people as a whole.

12 Anonymous, pp. 32-35

PLANTS USED IN MAKING VEGETABLE DYES

1. ACTINEA, SEVERAL-FLOWERED
2. ACTINEA, SINGLE-FLOWERED
3. ADLER
4. BEE PLANT, ROCKY MOUNTAIN
5. BITTERBALL
6. CACTUS, PRICKLY PEAR
7. CANYAIGRE
8. CELERY, WILD
9. CHAMIZO
10. CHOKECHERRY
11. CLAW, OWL'S
12. GRAPE, OREGON
13. IRONWOOD OR WILD PRIVET
14. JUNIPER, ONE-SEEDED
15. LARKSPUR, WILD PURPLE
16. LICHEN, GROUND
17. LUPINE, BLUE-FLOWERED
18. MAHOGANY, MOUNTAIN
19. OAK, GANBEL'S
20. PAINTBRUSH, INDIAN
21. OAK, SCRUB
22. PLUM, WILD
23. PINEDROP
24. RABBITBRUSH, SMALL
25. RABBIT, BIG
26. THISTLE, RUSSIAN

Glossary of Textile Terms

ANILINE. A colorless oily compound. The base from which many coal-tar dyes are made. In this publication the term is used to refer to commercial chemical dyes.

BATTEN. A sword-shaped piece of wood used to keep warp sets apart while a weft is inserted, and to beat the weft down into position. The word is both noun and verb.

BAYETA. The Spanish name for a cloth of English manufacture—baize—which was brought into the Southwest via Mexico and traded by the piece to the Indians.

BEADING. In textile terminology, beading does *not* mean the sewing of beads to cloth. It refers to the weaving of a narrow stripe in which tiny blocks of color alternate.

CARD (CARDER). A flat, rectangular paddle with a handle on one side and short metal teeth set in one surface. Wool fibers are separated and straightened by combing them between two cards.

"CHIEF" BLANKET. A man's or woman's shoulder blanket of distinctive design, shaped so that the longer dimension runs from side to side rather than from top to bottom.

COCHINEAL. A scarlet dye made from the dried, crushed bodies of little insects from Mexico, Java, and the Canary Islands. The dye used for red bayeta.

COMB (WEAVING COMB). A hand-like wooden tool used to force wefts down between warps prior to applying pressure with the batten.

DIAMOND STYLE. A design style popular in the Transition Period and characterized by the presence of small diamonds, triangles and oblique lines. Also called *serrate* style. (See p. 21.)

DOUBLE CLOTH (DOUBLE WEAVE). See *twill.*

DOUGIES. Coarse, handspun, wool wearing blankets. The word is a corruption of *Di-yu-ge,* the Navaho term for a soft, fluffy weave.

GANADO RED. A distinctive red characteristic of blankets and rugs woven around Ganado. A commercial chemical dye, it is noticeably darker than the red commonly found in other weaving centers.

GERMANTOWN YARN. Commercial American yarns colored by chemical dyes. Some early (ca. 1880) Germantown yarns were 3-ply, but ordinarily they are 4-ply.

Continued next page

HANDSPUN YARN. A single-ply yarn of native manufacture spun on the shaft-and-whorl spindle.

HEDDLE. A device for controlling a set of warps. It consists of a slender rod placed in horizontal position in front of the warps. String loops attached to the rod encircle selected warps. When the rod is pulled forward these warps are separated from the others, and a weft may be shot in behind them.

INDIGO. A dark blue dye made from any of several plants.

LAZY LINE. A slight, often nearly invisible, fault in the form of an oblique line sometimes found in Navaho blankets or rugs. It is created if the weaver carries her weft back and forth across one section of the warps instead of carrying it from edge to edge of the web in each pick. Adjoining sections are marked off in the finished piece by the oblique lines separating them. It is said the Navaho woman prefers to work in this manner when weaving a textile of greater width than her reach so that she need not shift her position with every weft.

LOOM. A frame on which warps are stretched for weaving. It is equipped with one or more heddles and a shed rod for controlling warp sets. The blanket loom of the Navaho is set upright on the ground. (Page 2.)

MANTA. The Spanish term for the blanket used by Pueblo Indian women as a shawl or wrap-around dress. Its greater dimension runs with the weft, or from side to side rather than top to bottom.

MOKI (MOQUI). A term formerly used for the Hopi Indians of northeastern Arizona.

OUTLINE STYLE. A design style popular in the early Rug Period (circa 1890). The distinguishing characteristic is the outlining of each small diamond or triangular figure with a narrow line of contrasting color.

PICK. A single length of weft.

PLAIN WEAVE. A weave in which single weft threads interlace over and under single warp threads.

PLY. A twist of yarn. *Single-ply*: fibers twisted into a single, continuous thread by one spinning. *Two-ply*: two threads plied, or twisted, together into a heavier yarn.

PUEBLO INDIANS. The term, of Spanish origin, used for Indians living in settled, agricultural villages in the Rio Grande Valley, Western New Mexico and Northeastern Arizona.

Continued next page

PULLED WARP. See *wedge weave.*

SADDLE BLANKET. A small blanket designed for use under a horse's saddle. These are of two standard sizes: single saddle blanket, 30" by 30"; and double saddle blanket, 30" by 60".

SAXONY YARN. A three-ply wool yarn colored with vegetable dyes. Manufactured in Saxony, Germany, it was imported into the Southwest in the middle 1800's.

SERAPE. A blanket about 3 or 4 feet wide and 6 or 7 long, commonly woven and used by Mexicans. This shape was copied by Pueblo and Navaho weavers. (Amsden, pp. 101-102.)

SERRATE STYLE. See *diamond style.*

SHED ROD. A stick passed behind a selected set of warps by means of which these warps may be forced forward to create a shed for the passage of a weft.

SPINDLE. A device for twisting fibers together into one continuous strand, or thread. The Navaho spindle consists of two parts: a slender shaft about 2 feet long and pointed at the ends; and a disk-shaped wooden weight, or whorl, near one end, through which the shaft passes.

STORM PATTERN. A distinctive pattern found principally on rugs from the Tuba City area. (See p. 40.)

TAPESTRY. A weave in which wefts are battened so closely together as to conceal warps.

TERRACED STYLE. The characteristic design style of the Classic Period. Terraced patterns are based on right-angled figures.

TWILL WEAVES may be recognized by the diagonal ribs on the surface of the cloth. These are made by floating wefts in echelon over one, two, or more warps at a time. The ribs may be arranged in herringbone or diamond patterns.

WARP. The yarn stretched on the loom preparatory to weaving.

WEDGE WEAVE. A novelty weave found in some blankets of the Transition Period. By means of this weave patterns of zigzag lines were made. The warp was forced out of its normal vertical position, and the edges of the blanket were "scalloped." (See p. 26.)

WEFT. The yarn woven over and under warps at right angles to them.

YEI. A Navaho divinity.

Supplementary References

AMSDEN, CHARLES AVERY

1949. Navaho weaving. University of New Mexico Press. Albuquerque.

ANONYMOUS.

1960. So you want to buy a Navaho rug. Indian Life volume 39, number 1. Ward Anderson Printing Company. Albuquerque.

BARTLETT, KATHARINE.

1950. Present trends in weaving on the western Navaho Reservation. Plateau, volume 23, number 1. Museum of Northern Arizona. Flagstaff.

BRYAN, NONABAH G. AND YOUNG, STELLA

1940. Navaho native dyes. Indian Handcraft Series number 2, Education Division, United States Office of Indian Affairs. Washington

DOUGLAS, FREDERIC H.

1951. Navaho wearing blankets. Leaflet number 113. Department of Indian Art, Denver Art Museum. Denver.

1953. Southwestern weaving materials. Leaflet number 116. Department of Indian Art, Denver Art Museum. Denver.

JAMES, GEORGE WHARTON.

1920. Indian blankets and their makers. A. C. McClurg and Company. Chicago.

MERA, H. P.

No date. Navaho textile arts. Laboratory of Anthropology. Santa Fe.

1949. The Alfred I. Barton collection of Southwestern textiles. San Vicente Foundation, Inc. Santa Fe.

REICHARD, GLADYS.

1936. Navajo shepherd and weaver. J. J. Augustin. New York.

Acknowledgements

The history of weaving among the Navaho Indians of Arizona and New Mexico, from its origin, probably around 1700 A.D. until the 1930's, has been well told by Charles Amsden and others. (See list of references, p. 46.) There is no single adequate reference on events of the past quarter century, however, and a really detailed study of contemporary weaving remains to be written. The facts presented in Chapters IV and V of this booklet were gathered largely through interviews with dealers, traders, government officials and anthropologists familiar with the current picture. I wish to thank all those who contributed information, particularly the following: Mr. and Mrs. Gilbert Maxwell of Farmington, New Mexico; Mr. Al Packard, Chaparral Trading Post, Santa Fe; Mrs. Allison Dodge, Fort Wingate, New Mexico; Mr. Russ L. Lingruen and Mr. Ned Hatathli of Window Rock; Miss Katharine Bartlett and Mr. Barton Wright, Museum of Northern Arizona, Flagstaff. Thanks are due also to Mr. Royal Hassrick of the Denver Art Museum and Mr. Stewart Peckham of the Laboratory of Anthropology in Santa Fe for making available their Navaho blanket collection for comparison with certain of the older Heard pieces.

Kate Peck Kent
March, 1961

Cover photograph courtesy.................. George C. Hight
Gallup, New Mexico

Photography ....Tyree Trobaugh
Globe, Arizona

Illustrations...James V. Parker
Curator of Education — Heard Museum

Consultant...H. Thomas Cain
Curator — Heard Museum